Naturally Delicious

Ideas-Tips-Recipes

Hormone & Chemical-Free, Non-GMO, Organic Food Made Easy

Rebekah S. Mead RN, MSN Ed.

Naturally Delicious

Ideas – Tips -- Recipes

Hormone & Chemical Free, Non-GMO, Organic Food Made Easy

ISBN: 9798612306245

Rebekah Mead

This book is dedicated to my darling Millie and Maggie Mead. Some of the best times of my life have been spent baking and cooking with my granddaughters. Sometimes memories make the best recipes.

Rebekah Mead

CONTENTS

Preface:

Why I Eat Hormone & Chemic-free, Non-GMO, Organic Food

I grew up on a small farm within a farming community. What my parents used to call food, which was long before the mid- 1990's, is today dubbed *hormone & chemical-free, non-GMO, organic produce and meat.* Our eggs, milk, butter, and meat came from farm animals that were not given growth hormones or antibiotics, and they ate organic grains.

Over the past two decades, I was friends with a few naturalists who made me aware of changes in our food supply. As a healthcare professional, I began to recognize how few people are aware of how much food sold in supermarkets had changed since 1994— the time when the first legislation was passed to allow Genetical Modified Organisms (GMO) to be sold as food. Our current chemical cuisine has been a covert evolution over the past twenty-five years. Changing our diet back will not be an overnight endeavor, but for the sake of our plant and personal health, it is one that must be undertaken.

When asked by other people what I eat, if I am avoiding all food additives/chemicals, GMO, pharma-culture food, I tell them I eat everything I used to eat. I simply avoid everything that may put me at higher risk for illnesses based on my personal health. For instance, I am a female over forty-five, so I avoid excessive phosphates that are routinely added in various forms to most processed foods. I avoid this because phosphorus attaches to the same receptor sites in our body as calcium, but more readily. Too much phosphorus in a diet can lead to low-bone-density and osteoporosis.

Instead of chemical pizza or GMO fish, I eat chemical-free, Non-GMO, organic pizza, and wild-caught fish. I cook with unprocessed, non-GMO, high gluten flour-- ah, yes, I said HIGH GLUTEN, because gluten is grain protein. By using only non-GMO, I am assured there are no foreign genes that may be causing allergies or other health problems. For example, 90% of all soy sold and used by food-producers is GMO with unknown genes added. GMO soy has a high risk of allergies and many other health problems. What is sold as unprocessed, Non-GMO, organic, high-gluten flour today, used to be sold as plain old flour in supermarkets many years ago. That was before the modern chemical-cuisine evolution, and before flour was stripped of all its nutrients and then enriched with chemicals to add texture and put some nutritional value back in.

Back when real flour was sold in supermarkets, our old recipes turned out great with wonderful flavor and texture. Flour back then was high in gluten and did not need chemicals to replace the nutrients that are now processed out.

Once I realized how the food-industry had changed, I switched my diet to real food. And when I did, all my health problems disappeared, and my homemade meals returned to their wonderful flavor with the texture I remember from my past.

People who doubt that the miracles of real-food can reverse diseases and ailments are not looking at the causes of their ailments. As an Environment Health & Safety Nurse, I learned to perform Root-Cause-Analysis and then remove the agents that put employees at risk for disease or injury. I soon realized that by removing the agent that causes the symptoms, we are not healing the problem, but rather preventing the side-effects.

In other words, when you over-exert yourself and tear a muscle, your medical provider will likely instruct you to stop using the injured body part. Let it rest. But if diagnosed with pancreatic lesions or any Irritable Bowel Disease, seldom will a medical provider instruct you to stop consuming ingredients that cause those symptoms—for example, very few medical providers will warn patients to stop consuming High Fructose Corn Syrup (HFCS) for a month or so to see if lesions improve or go away because HFCS is known to increase risk for pancreatic lesions (Topsakal, 2016) (Charrez, 2015). Or, stop consuming dairy products that contain carrageenan because carrageenan increases the risk for Crohn's disease and Irritable Bowel symptoms (David, 2018). Instead, you may be told to avoid entire food groups that contain vital nutrients that are necessary for good health when, in fact, it's a food-additives causing the problems.

There are many hormones, chemicals/food additives and GMO (unknown DNA) added to processed foods today that didn't exist when I was growing up. HFCS and carrageenan are only two of the more than 80,000 alterations made to our food today. The reason I write about these two is that I personally noticed a huge change in my health upon eliminating them from my diet in addition to avoiding all farm-animal products that come from animals given antibiotics and/or hormones.

The purpose of writing this book is to increase consumer awareness, to inform and help homemakers prepare nutritious and delicious meals for their friends and family at an affordable price. I am sharing many of my favorite recipes, but the main point I want to make is that conventional ingredients are not what they used to be. If you are using one of your grandmother's old recipes and it is not turning out the way it should, try switching to all Non-GMO and Organic ingredients--- I think you will be shocked at the difference it makes.

Disclaimer: Product brands shown in pictures are not an endorsement of these products. These are brands of products that I use. Some are the only organic brand available in my area. Any Hormone & Chemical Free, Non-GMO, organic brands can be used.

Chapter 1: Where's the Beef?

Do you remember the commercial, "Where's the Beef?" It was over thirty years ago that this commercial accused its competitors of using too little beef in their burgers.

Wow! Have times changed. Today, in modern times, processed meat products have even less meat added. Many of the processed products today state they are made with meat when, in fact, they contain little or no real meat. Instead, these products contain many chemical-fillers with additional chemicals that help disguise the imitation meat. One such deceiving way of fooling consumers is the use of a filler called *Vegetable Textured Protein (VTP)*. Mechanically Separated Meat (MSM) or Mechanically Recovered Meat (MRM) is another way that food processors are fooling the consumer.

I don't know about you, but I stay away from anything that discloses in its ingredient panel the use of VTP, MSM, or MRM instead of actual meat.

Why? You may ask.

My response to this is another question. What exactly is "VTP?" If it is soy, 94% of all soy used in American products has unknown DNA—it is GMO with no information on the label informing the consumer about what those foreign genes are or where they came from. If the VTP is comprised of chemicals, again, the potential side-effects, regardless of whether I eat one or more servings, are unknown to me.

And, what exactly is MSM & MRM?

The end product of MSM and MRM is made by forcing scraps from pork, mutton, beef, chicken, or turkey, under high pressure through a sieve to separate the bone from the remaining tissue after the good cuts of meat have been removed. This entails pureeing or grinding the remaining carcass, after the manual removal of meat from the bones, and then forcing the slurry through a sieve under pressure. This puree includes bone, bone marrow, skin, nerves, blood vessels, lymph nodes, and tumors remaining on the bones. This is a blend consisting mostly of tissues not generally considered meat, along with a tiny amount of actual meat (muscle tissue). According to at least one statistical review, there is a significant difference in protein, cholesterol, ash, iron, and calcium content in a cut of meat compared to that found in the MSM or MRM. Also, there is a higher risk of infectious contamination in the MSM & MRM meat products (EFSA, 1993).

The way I feel about labeling is, if our legislators will not pass laws that require food producers to inform us what is in the foods being sold in the USA, then as an informed consumer, I only buy what I know is safe—hence, hormone & chemical-free, Non-GMO, organic food.

Why Does Organic Food Cost More?

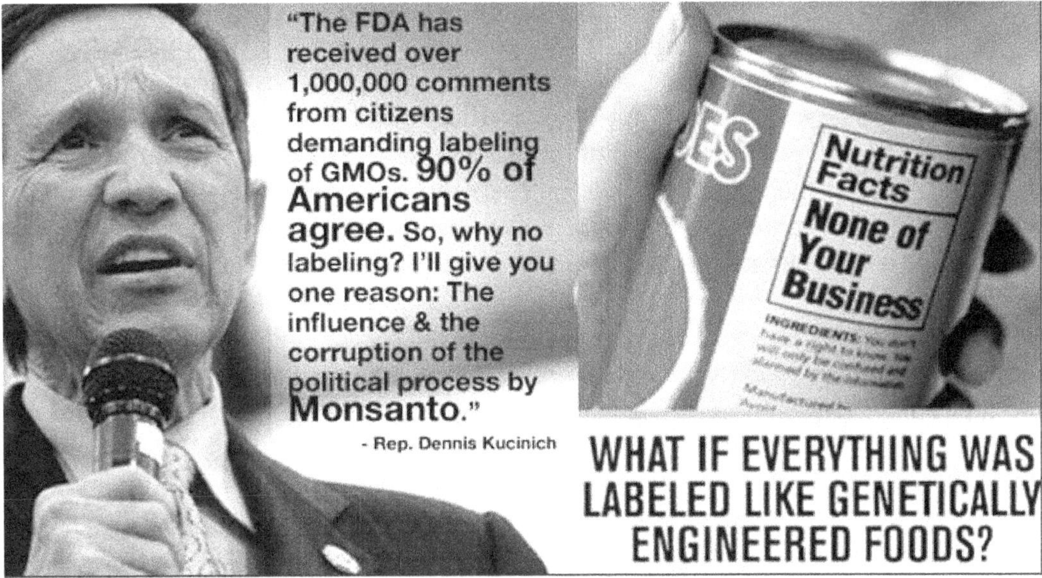

1.   Mistakenly, many Americans believe there is no nutritional difference between organic and conventional items. Most Americans I speak with think organic food is too expensive. However, aside from the difference in composition, which is why most conventional foods must be enriched with chemical nutrients, there are significant reasons why supermarkets charge more for organic food.

2.   Meat, poultry, and seafood raised with growth hormones and DNA from larger animals take less time to raise. Also, less meat is used in processed meals because they use a very small portion of meat, poultry, or seafood supplemented with *Vegetable Textured Protein* that makes it appear to have more meat than there really is.

3.   Organic foods derived from animals cost more than their conventional counterparts because conventional meat and seafood often use *sodium tripolyphosphate* to make old meat and seafood look fresh. Meat retailers may also glue bits and pieces of old meat from various sources together with *transglutaminase* to fool the consumer into thinking they are getting a fresh cut of meat or seafood.

4.

Organic growers are unfairly burdened with regulations that conventional growers do not incur.

- Organic certification is time-consuming and flat out expensive for many growers and handlers. Not only are first-time certification costs steep, averaging around $700 to $1,200 per operation, but there are other certification costs involved as well. Some of the major certification costs include renewal certification costs, education, suitable organic land, and livestock from organic origins, organic seed, and special processing equipment, all of which are scrutinized (Wozencraft, 2019).

- Conventional growers are self-regulated. They monitor themselves with no additional costs.

- Organic food producers don't use the same readily available cheap fillers, additives, flavors, and preservatives as conventional food producers do. There's a long list of harmful ingredients not allowed in organic food. This means organic producers must use less harmful but often more ingredients. It obviously costs less to use synthetic food items, so conventional food companies get a real financial break that organic companies don't.

5.   Unfair Subsidies: Food prices are influenced by government subsidies. Conventional, junk food is subsidized much more than organics and healthier crops. In 2008, the House Appropriations Committee found that spending on farm subsidies totaled $7.5 billion annually, which only $15 million was designated to organic and local food programs combined (Wozencraft, 2019).

When agribusiness crops receive a subsidy, it lowers the cost consumers pay for the end food item. Since conventional food gets the bulk of subsidies, **organic prices appear higher than they really are because conventional food prices are way lower than they should be.**

In fact, most government-funded subsidies are used to finance GMO commodity crops such as corn and soybeans that are often processed into food additives like high fructose corn syrup and vegetable oil and then used in junk food (The Cornucopia Institute , 2010).

6.   The more consumers buy, the more a company will produce, and the more they produce, the lower their prices will fall. This is supply and demand. When more consumers by only organics, there will be more demand, enabling organic operations to scale up. In turn, this will lower costs. But as long as consumers flock to cheap, toxic food, that's what companies will produce.

7.   Hidden Costs Many Americans Fail to Recognize

- $ Environmental land, soil, and water pollution. We pay for these costs through our tax dollars, not through our food budget (Chait, 2019).

- $ Conventional food production also costs more for pesticide manufacturing and disposal. Pesticides, a known health risk, are abundant in conventional food, so when we eat pesticide-filled foods, we rack up bigger bills for medical expenses as well (Chait, 2019).

- $ Organics provide better animal welfare, promote rural development, and help increase jobs — issues at which the conventional food production system fails miserably.

- $ Organics help save pollinators: Conventional food used harmful biocides to kill bees, butterflies, and other creatures. Without pollinators, the green earth will die, and global warming will kill the rest of life on this planet.

- $ Organic crops have no patents. Seeds and soil are free to use compared to GMO seeds that require GMO chemicals in patented soil to grow.

(CALPRIG, 2011)

America is facing an obesity epidemic – one that's hitting children especially hard. Childhood obesity rates have tripled over the last three decades, with one in five kids aged 6 to 11 now obese. These increases in obesity rates will translate into kids who are at greater risk for heart disease and diabetes, undermining the health of our country and driving up medical costs by hundreds of billions of dollars.

The rise in childhood obesity has many causes, but one of the most important is the increased prevalence of high-fat, heavily sweetened junk food. And shockingly, American taxpayers are spending billions to subsidize junk food ingredients, making the problem worse. Between 1995 and 2010, American taxpayers spent over $260 billion in agricultural subsidies. Most subsidies went to the country's largest farming operations, mainly to grow just a few commodity crops, including GMO corn and GMO soybeans While dairy and livestock receive a stipend of federal support, it is the commodity crops that get the lion's share of the subsidies.

Most of these commodity crops are not simply eaten as-is. Among other uses, food manufacturers process them into additives like high fructose corn syrup and vegetable oils that provide a cheap dose of sweetness and fat to a wide variety of junk food products. Thus, Americans' tax dollars are directly subsidizing junk food ingredients.

Between 1995 and 2010, $16.9 billion in tax dollars subsidized four common food additives - corn syrup, high fructose corn syrup, corn starch, and soy oils (which are frequently processed further into hydrogenated vegetable oils).

Outside of commodity crops, other agricultural products receive very little in federal subsidies. Since 1995, taxpayers spent only $262 million subsidizing apples, which is the only significant federal subsidy of fresh fruits or vegetables.

If these agricultural subsidies went directly to consumers to allow them to purchase food, each of America's 144 million taxpayers would be given $7.36 to spend on junk food and 11 cents with which to buy apples each year – enough to buy 19 Twinkies but less than a quarter of one Red Delicious apple apiece.

The fact that so many tax dollars are being wasted on junk food demonstrates the need to reform national agricultural subsidies and end this wasteful spending.

It's frightening when you see a cheap jar of conventional GMO peanut butter loaded with chemicals, or a bag of conventional GMO apples that contain *who-knows-what-genes* sitting right next to higher-priced organic varieties, but once you look at the whole story, it's easy to see that organic foods offer benefits and long-term money savings that conventional food never will.

Chapter 2: Preferred Ingredients

Pharmed foods created in laboratories may look like organic food, but it sure does not taste or cook-up like Mother Nature's organic ingredients.

In general, when I food-shop, I look for:

1. Products with fewest ingredients: For example:

    A. Ice cream made with 3 ingredients: Milk, sugar, and vanilla

    B. Organic butter made from organic milk

    C. Organic canned tomatoes

2. Foods that contain only organic plant or animal products

3. Preferably certified organic or at least Non-GMO

4. Fewest chemicals/food additives

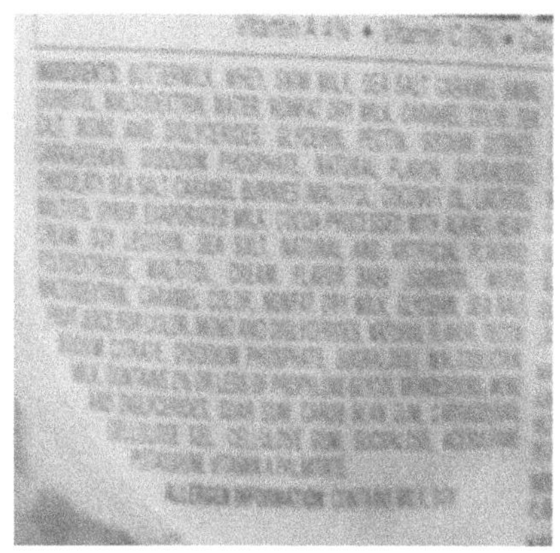

Choosing Ice Cream
I choose ice creams with the fewest natural ingredients. Ice cream and other dairy products containing lots of chemicals make me feel bloated and gassy. Occasionally I get hives from these products. But, when I eat natural ice cream, I am not afflicted with any side-effects.

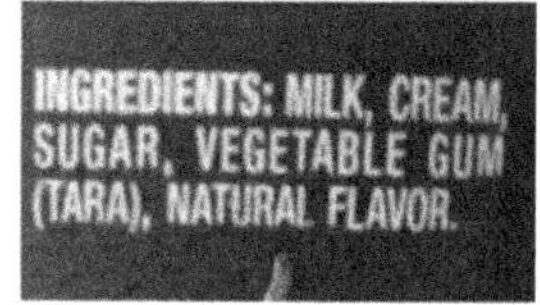

5. Food with NO:

   A. Carrageenan

   B. High Fructose Corn Syrup

   C. Red Dye (especially #40); Yellow Dye; Blue Dye

   D. Aspartame or Acesulfame

   E. Phosphates of any kind

   F. Fat-free foods that substitute high calories additives

6. No Vegetables and fruits with pesticide residue—PLU codes that start with #3 or #4 are a no no for me

7. Organic ketchup, oils, and other condiments

The Basic Ingredients I Use Are:

A variety of Non-GMO, organic oils

Eggs from free-range outdoor, Non-GMO fed chicken

Organic mayonnaise made with eggs from cage-free chickens fed Non-GMO food

100% heavy whipping cream or heavy whipping cream with no carrageenan

Buttermilk with no carrageenan or dyes

Truvia Blend – 1/3 organic sugar and 2/3 stevia or Stevia leaves from my garden

Organic sugar and 10x sugar

I buy organic fruits and vegetables from local farmers when in season

Non-GMO, organic high gluten flour

♥ I like the flavor and health benefits of
  Stevia blends. They are:
  ✓ low in calories
  ✓ lowers blood pressure
  ✓ lowers blood sugar

♥ Truvia is ¾'s Stevia and ¼ Non-GMO sugar. When substituting
  Truvia for sugar in any recipe- use ½ the amount of sugar (i.e., 1 c
  sugar = ½ c Truvia)

♥ When substituting Truvia in recipes, you are getting 1/8 the calories
  from sugar because you substitute half the quantity of regular sugar.

♥ If you prefer sugar when cooking the recipes in this book, double the
  amt of Stevia (i.e., 1 Tbsp of Truvia = 2 Tbsp Organic Sugar)

Chapter 3: TIPS

♥ Organic food can attract pests. When displaying fresh fruit on my

counter or dining room table, I add a sprig of organic mint and/or citronella plant leaves to the bowl. These herbs repel fruit-flies, ants, and other bugs even long after the mint or citronella leaves dry up.

♥ When I see organic high gluten flour in my travels, I buy 20 – 40 pounds and keep it in my freezer. This way, it stays fresh for a long time.

♥ Gluten is grain protein. Its protein absorbs fluid, which gives baked goods its elasticity & texture. When gluten (the grain's protein) is processed-out of the flour, all that is left us a powdery byproduct! Homemade cookies, bread, and other baked goods made from gluten-free flour cannot rise and will lack texture unless other chemicals are used to improve the texture.

The composition of processed flour is very different than high-gluten flour. Older cookbooks published before the 1990s assume the cook is using unprocessed flour.

Do you lack cooking skills?

OR

Is it the ingredients you use?

♥ Chemicals used to remove nutrient-rich gluten from processed flour are high-risk for allergies and digestive system problems.

Unprocessed Non-GMO grain contains valuable nutrients necessary for good health: Protein, fiber, folic acid, and niacin (Dannie, 2018), (Martin, Geisel, Maresch, Krieger, & Stein, 2013) (Di Nardo G1, 2019). Several studies and guidelines in adults demonstrated that the intake of dietary fiber provided by a gluten-free diet is inadequate for proper digestion (Kupper, 2005).

♥ If you think you can't afford organic food--- shop around. The same organic product can be over-priced at one store while another is selling the same brand for half that price.

If you think organic food is expensive,

wait until you get your medical bills for treating all of the side-effects your chemical cuisine diet causes.

What you save in medical fees can buy a lot of organic food.

♥ Organic onions used to make me cry—the tears ran down my face as the aroma burned my eyes. One day, many years ago, I heard a news-reporter announce that improved-onions were coming that would no longer cause teary eyes! I anxiously awaited the *improved* onion that did not make me cry (as promised) and eagerly bought a bag as soon as they came to my local market-place. Much to my disappointment, not only did they lack the tearful aroma, but they also lacked any flavor in my recipes!

I then cried for the days when I used to taste onions in my food. I finally grew my own organic onion and bought a truly organic onion in the store that made my eyes teared up like they used to, but now they are tears of joy. I love the taste of a real onion.

♥ If your organic peanut butter is dry and hard in the refrigerator, mix some with peanut (or other) oil to soften it. I also soften it with applesauce, fresh berries, fresh bananas, or jelly by simply putting a serving size into my Nutra bullet. It comes out easy to spread on a slice of bread.

⊘ I use organic lemon and orange peels in various recipes. I never use fruit that has the sticker (Product-Look-Up code / PLU) starting with #3 or #4, because these fruits can be saturated in pesticides and rodenticides, which are sprayed to repel or harm pests. Hence whatever harm it does to pests, it can also do to humans. Many biocides are hormone and enzyme disruptors.

When more consumers buy only organic products, the demand will increase, enabling organic operations to scale up. That, in turn, will lower costs. When consumers flock to cheap, toxic food, that's what food-manufacturers produce. Buying only organic is an effective way of saving the planet and reducing healthcare expenses. Its an action everyone can ban together on to bring about change.

Does this milk taste a little funny to you?

Chapter 4: Hormone-free, Chemical-Free, Non-GMO, organic Recipes

Some of My ★ ★★★ Recipes

Anyone who remembers my recipe index-file or cookbooks since the 1970s knows I mark my recipes with stars—four-stars being terrific, three is very good, two is okay once in a while but needs some work, but it has potential. One star was reserved for cookbooks only to note it was tried and not any good.

As great and dependable as my recipes were back then, artificial and GMO ingredients ruin the way these recipes turn out. It is frustrating and a waste of precious time & money when a recipe flops. What I learned through persistence and a lot of research is that the key to nutritious and delicious meals every time is in the quality of the ingredients. Homemade recipes must be made with real, Non-GMO, organic ingredients.

16

Beverages

Mint w/ Stevia Iced Tea

I grow mint and stevia plants in my garden.

½ - ¾ Quart of cold water

Sprig or handful of mint leaves

Sprig or handful of Stevia leaves (Optional)

Your favorite teabags

(fresh ground ginger and/or fresh lemon juice optional)

In a large pot, bring cold water, mint, and Stevia leaves to a rolling boil.

Let boil for 5 minutes.

Remove from heat, add your favorite tea bags; let seep 5- 10 minutes (or however strong you want your iced tea).

Remove tea bags and leaves. Let sit until room temperature, then pour into glass jugs. Refrigerate until cold.

Low Cal Raspberry Iced Tea

4 -5 Tea Bags (Green tea works well)

1 gallon of water divided

1/2 cup Truvia or fresh stevia leaves

12 oz organic Raspberries

Juice of 1/2 Lemon

Boil about 3/4 gallon of water in a large pot. After rolling boil, remove from heat and add teabags.

Let seep 5 minutes or so

Two Options:

1. In the meantime, blend 8 oz of raspberries with a cup of water in a Nutra Bullet or blender. Strain to remove seeds. Add the reserved water and Stevia and boil until thickened. Add remaining raspberries and stir lightly. Let cool, blend in lemon juice. Add to the tea in a large pot.

2. In the meantime, in quart size pot with remaining water, add raspberries, Stevia, and boil until thickened stirring constantly. Remove from heat and cool. Add lemon juice and then pour it into the iced tea.

Let cool and pour into glass jugs

♥ Just make the raspberry and lemon mixture. Pour into an ice cube tray and freeze. This adds a great flavor to a glass of water or iced tea.

♥ Freeze additional Raspberries, blueberries, strawberries, and add to Raspberry iced tea when ready to serve. Berries make flavorful and decorative ice cubes.

Blackberry Iced Tea

1 Gallon water

3 family-size tea bags or 5 regular tea bags

16 oz fresh organic blackberries, divided

1/2 cup Truvia or handful of fresh Stevia leaves

¼ cup fresh lemon juice

Optional for serving

      4 slices fresh organic lemon

      4 sprigs fresh organic mint

      Freeze some blackberries

Garnish with lemon wedges, fresh blackberries, fresh mint

In a medium-size pan, mash 1½ cups blackberries; stir in Stevia and lemon juice.

Heat to thicken, then let cool to room temperature; refrigerate about 3 hours.

In the meantime, in a large pot, boil water let boil for 3-5 minutes, remove from heat, and add tea bags. Let steep for 3 to 4 minutes; remove tea bags.

Strain blackberry mixture through a fine-mesh sieve into a pitcher; discard solids. Add to tea.

When ready to serve, stir in blackberries, lemon slices, and mint

Coffee Frappe

Ice cube tray filled with strong coffee

6 oz cold coffee

3 oz organic milk

2 Tablespoons organic Maple syrup (or 1 Tbsp maple syrup and 1 tsp Stevia)

Dash of Non-GMO Carmel syrup

Put all ingredients, including ice cubes, into bullet and blend.

♥ Alternate ingredients: Instead of caramel, add cinnamon

♥ If unsweetened is desired, eliminate maple and caramel syrup

Orange Milk Shake

Organic Vanilla Ice cream (with no carrageenan, high fructose corn syrup, corn syrup or other chemicals)

Organic orange

Blend both ingredients in a Nutra-Bullet or blender

Christmas Wine Punch

3 cups fresh squeezed or bottled organic orange juice

¾ cup Truvia sugar blend or 1 ½ cups sugar

1 ½ cups squeezed organic lemon juice

1 – 4/5 quart chilled sauterne

½ cup brandy

1 – 4/5 quart bottle chilled Asti Spumante champagne

1 cup of frozen whole organic strawberries

Organic orange slices

Combine orange juice, sugar, and lemon juice. Stir until sugar dissolved. Chill for at least
4 hours or overnight.

When ready to serve, pour orange juice mixture into a large punch bowl, stir in sauterne,
and brandy. Gently pour in the champagne and garnish with frozen strawberries
and orange slices.

Memories Make the Best Recipes

This was one of the first recipes I collected after getting married. I made it for parties and every Christmas. It was served in a large punch bowl at my in-laws 40th wedding anniversary. Our Minister Reverend Bulhour loved it a lot, but Mrs. Bulhour insisted he not drink too much.

Bread

Bread-Machine White Bread

I love my bread machine. It takes two minutes to put ingredients into the maker and push a button. 3-4 hours later (or overnight), I have a nutrient-rich, chemical-free loaf of bread.

Warning: If your machine is not producing a fluffy, tasty loaf of bread, don't give up-- it's either the ingredients you are using (processed powdery flour vs. high gluten flour; pharmed eggs vs. farmed organic eggs; dairy diluted with water and carrageenan vs. 100% buttermilk, milk, butter, etc..) or it may be a bad recipe. I had one recipe that I tried in three different Bread Maker machines, and all three came out as a hard lump of dough.

My favorite Breadmaker recipe

1 egg

1 cup buttermilk

4 Tbsp soft butter

3 cups high-gluten flour

1 Tbsp Truvia – Stevia with sugar mixture

1 tsp salt

1 ½ tsp bread-baking yeast

Put all ingredients into the bread maker in order listed above. Do not let yeast touch
     liquid. Room temperature ingredients work best.

Makes 1 ½ load size, choose the darkness of your choice, and start.

♥ **Breadcrumbs** – blend slice of bread in a bullet or blender. Add seasonings if desired.

Popovers

Very easy and flavorful

1 cup high-gluten flour (does not rise if processed flour used)

1 cup of organic milk

1 egg

1 tsp salt

Preheat oven at 425 F

Using a fork, blend until all lumps are gone.

Using a cupcake pan, grease each cup with olive, avocado or pecan oil

Fill each cup about ½ full

Bake for 15 minutes

Lower oven temperature to 350 F and cook for 15 – 20 minutes longer until golden brown

♥ Great addition to any meal, serve with butter.

♥ Centers are hollow; therefore, they can be filled with Bavarian cream and fruit.

Corn Fritters

1 cup plus 2 tsp flour

¼ tsp baking powder

1 egg

½ cup kernel corn (boiled and cut from the cob)

½ cup cream-style corn

2 Tbsp chopped green pepper (optional)

Mix ingredients together

Heat oil (peanut, avocado, or other cooking oil). Drop 1/8 or ¼ cup size corn fritter mixture into the hot oil, fry until golden brown. Turn during frying.

Yeast cakes

1 cup of flour

2 ½ tsp yeast

1 cup of warm water

1 tsp salt

Thoroughly blend all ingredients together. Cover with a warm towel and let rise in a warm place overnight. When ready to grill them, beat the risen dough down. Pour or spoon enough batter onto a hot griddle with butter or oil of choice. Fry like a pancake

♥ Serve with butter

♥ I make these yeast cakes to serve as Mexican tortillas- stuffed with cheese, grilled peppers and onions and whatever else, and serve with my favorite salsa, sour cream, and guacamole

Memories Make the Best Recipes

This is my father's recipe. He explained how his mother made this for him during the Great Depression. I grew up eating these for breakfast and thinking they were a delicacy. In retrospect, I now realize they were a depression food-- my grandmother made them during an era in Philadelphia, Pa. when there was a shortage in food.

Amish Potato Rolls

2 eggs

1/3 cup sugar

2 tsp salt

6 Tbsp soft butter

1 cup leftover mashed potatoes

2 ½ tsp instant yeast

¾ cup lukewarm water (if using freshly boiled potatoes, use the water)

4 ¼ cup high-gluten flour

Mix all ingredients together

Place in a greased bowl

Let rise for 90 minutes or until doubled in size

Gently deflate dough; divide into 16 large balls/rolls or 24 small rolls

Place on greased (' x 13" pan

Let rise 2 hours

Preheat oven to 350 F

Bake 20 – 25 minutes

Zucchini Bread

My sister-in-law Denise and I used to grow zucchini in our gardens. This was Carmen's, her mother's, recipe which I adapted slightly by using Truvia and carrots.

3 cups sifted flour

1 tsp salt

1 tsp baking soda

1 tsp baking powder

1 Tbsp cinnamon

3 eggs

¾ cup Truvia sugar (Stevia and sugar blend)

1 cup organic shortening or solid coconut oil

2 medium zucchini shredded

2 medium carrots shredded (optional)

1 Tbsp grated lemon peel (always use organic lemons to avoid pesticide residue)

1 tsp vanilla

(Optional ½ cup of chopped nuts)

Preheat oven 350 F

Sift flour, salt, baking soda, baking powder, and cinnamon together and set aside

Beat eggs lightly with mixer then blend in sugar and oil until light a fluffy

Stir in sugar, zucchini, carrots, lemon rind, and vanilla. (and nuts if desired)

Grease two 8" x 4" bread pans. Pour batter into each

Bake for 50 minutes

Raspberry & Cheese Danish

As you can see, eating organic does not involve any sacrifice.

1 package of Crescent Rolls

4 ounces of organic cream cheese

¼ cup confectioner's sugar

½ cup fresh berries or jam

½ cup confectioner's sugar

2 tsp organic milk

Preheat oven as 375 F.

Line cookie sheet with parchment paper

In a bowl, beat cream cheese and ¼ cup confectioner's sugar until smooth/

Unroll crescent dough and separate into 4 rectangles: Seal perforations. Cut each rectangle in half, making 8 squares

Transfer squares onto the baking sheet lined with parchment paper. Spread 1 Tbsp or so of cream cheese mix on each square. Top with fresh berries or 1 Tbsp of jam.

Bring opposite corners of dough together over filling and pinch together.

Bake for 10 – 12 minutes—until golden brown.

Combine milk and remaining confectioner's sugar together. Drizzle over cooled pastry.

Serve immediately, or I put two in each sandwich bag and freeze them until ready to serve.

Memories Make the Best Recipes

John loves pastries with his coffee, which he now only uses Stevia to sweeten. One day I decided to look up the side-effects of the chemicals in his mini donuts. After writing out the list of ingredients, I realized there were 51 chemicals to look up, and worse yet, there were no real ingredients/ natural food.

Salads & Dressings

Potato Salad

5 large organic russet potatoes: Boiled, peeled or unpeeled as desired

1 Boiled fresh egg: From cage-free organic fed chickens

¾ cup Non-GMO / Organic Mayonnaise

2 Tbsp chopped sweet pickles: Experiment with different varieties—its spices up the

    recipe

2 Tbsp sweet pickle juice

1 Tbsp Vinegar: Non-GMO Apple cider

2 Tbsp chopped organic green pepper

2 Tbsp chopped organic onion

1 tsp Dijon mustard

½ tsp stevia or Truvia

1 ¼ tsp salt

Cut potatoes in half and then thinly slice each half. Slice egg into thin slices. Toss egg and potatoes together in a bowl.

Mix the rest of the ingredients together and pour over egg-potato mixture.

♥ I prefer organic potatoes because I save the water used to boil the potatoes to make soup or to boil other vegetables. ***I do not want boiled condensed pesticide-residue in my broth***

♥ Potato water enhances the flavor of other vegetables boiled in the same water

♥ Potato water can be frozen in ice-cube trays or saved in larger containers in the freezer to use as veggie broth in the future

Coleslaw

1 cup of shredded organic   carrots

2 cups organic crispy cabbage

½ organic green pepper diced

1/3 cup Non-GMO mayonnaise- from

    cage-free chickens

1 ½ cup Non-GMO sweet relish or

    pickles

1/3 medium-size organic onion

    grated

½ tsp salt

¼ - ½ tsp Stevia or Truvia

Mix vegetables together

Blend mayonnaise with rest of ingredients, pour over cabbage mixture and toss well.

Refrigerate at least half-an-hour. This coleslaw will keep for a few days.

Tuna Macaroni Salad

6 oz organic elbow macaroni

1 cup cubed cheddar cheese

7 oz can of wild-caught tuna

¾ cup chopped sweet Non-GMO pickles

½ cup chopped organic onion

1 cup Non-GMO mayonnaise – made from eggs from cage-free organic fed

    chickens

¾ tsp salt

¼ tsp pepper

2 crushed organic garlic cloves.

Cook macaroni and drain.

Mix cheese, tuna, pickles, and onion in a bowl and set aside

Mix the rest of the ingredients together well and pour over tuna mixture.

Cover and chill at least 2 hours. Best if made the day before.

Great salads start with fresh organic veggies from your garden

Honey French Dressing

½ cup Olive Oil

1/3 cup Organic Certified & Non-GMO Ketchup

1/8 cup Truvia or stevia

¼ cup apple cider vinegar

1 Tbsp organic lemon juice

½ tsp Dijon mustard

½ tsp paprika

½ tsp salt

½ tsp pepper

Blend all ingredients together. Pour into a jar and serve over salad.

Fresh Basil Tomato Dressing

14 oz Non-GMO organic canned diced tomato or 5 -6 organic Roma tomatoes diced

1/3 cup organic vinegar

1/3 cup chopped fresh organic basil

½ tsp chopped organic garlic

½ tsp salt

¼ tsp pepper

Mix ingredients together. Pour into a glass jar. Refrigerate before serving.

Honey Mustard Dressing

½ cup olive or avocado oil

1 cup of local honey

½ cup ground pepper or flavored pepper (raspberry mustard is very good)

1/3 cup Dijon mustard

1 small minced garlic clove

3 tsp lemon juice

Mix all ingredients together. Pour into a glass jar and refrigerate

Bleu Cheese Dressing

1/3 cup organic reduced-fat or whole milk

1 tsp white vinegar

5 oz bleu cheese crumbled

1/3 cup Non-GMO (no carrageenan) sour cream

¼ cup Non-GMO mayonnaise made with eggs from cage-free, organic-fed chickens

4 tsp white vinegar

¼ tsp chopped organic garlic

1/8 tsp ground pepper

Dash of salt

Mix milk and 1 tsp vinegar together. Let sit for 5 – 10 minutes.

Add cheese- mash with a fork,

Add the rest of the ingredients. Put into a glass jar and refrigerate for at least 4 hours.

Italian Dressing

½ cup Non-GMO oil such as olive, avocado or pecan

3 Tbsp wine vinegar

1 Tbsp seasoned salt

½ tsp Truvia or stevia

1/8 tsp ground pepper

¼ tsp paprika

Blend all ingredients together and pour over a fresh salad.

Can make 2 -4 x recipe and pour it into a glass jar. Refrigerate and serve with salad.

Blackberry Tarragon Salad Dressing

1 cup Non-GMO organic blackberries

½ cup wine vinegar

1 cup oil – olive or pecan oil taste great

½ cup plain yogurt (Non-GMO with NO carrageenan or high fructose corn syrup)

2 Tbsp local honey

½ tsp salt

1 Tbsp fresh organic tarragon

Mix berries and vinegar in a blender. Press through a sieve to remove seeds. Add the rest of the ingredients. Pour into a jar and refrigerate.

Spinach Salad

10 -16 oz. Fresh Organic spinach

11 oz can Non-GMO mandarin oranges drained or fresh oranges

½ cup sliced organic onions

1 small organic red pepper sliced

** Organic Roasted Pecans optional – Recipe below

Mix vegetables and oranges together (and pecans if desired)

Serve with Honey mustard dressing or Blackberry Tarragon Salad dressing

Pour dressing over salad when ready to serve

** Organic Roasted Pecans optional

1 cup pecans cut in half	¼ tsp ground cinnamon
½ tsp soft butter	¾ tsp salt
1 Tbsp Truvia Brown Sugar	¼ tsp cayenne pepper
1 Tbsp organic maple syrup	

Preheat oven at 350 F.

Line baking sheet with parchment paper

Place pecans on a baking sheet and toast for 10 minutes

While nuts are roasting, mix together butter, sugar, syrup, and seasonings in a bowl

Remove pecans from oven and drop individually into the mixture—making sure to
coat each.

Return to the baking dish with parchment paper and bake an additional 10 minutes.

Garden Salad

I grew up in New Jersey, and believe me, there's nothing like a Jersey Tomato! An organic tomato, grown in organic clay soil and fertilized with natural farm-animal manure, is the sweetest, most tangy tomato on earth. I thought the days of a real tomato were gone until I bought a packet of organic seeds from the Organic Seed Exchange and grew them in organic soil with organic fertilizer from a local farmer. Wow! For the first time in years, I ate a juicy, tangy, real tomato. Boy, real tomatoes are incredible!

John says I look like a grandma showing pictures of the grandkids when I pull out my phone to show pics of my garden. I got thousands more for anyone who wants to see them!

Meat

Try your old family favorite recipes using 100% organic meat and ingredients

Meatballs

Makes 16 meatballs – 8 servings

1 ½ lb. of organic ground beef

3 medium organic garlic cloves -crushed

¼ to ½ tsp fennel seeds crushed

Dash of pepper

½ cup organic grated carrot

1/3 cup chopped organic parsley

2 organic eggs

1 ¼ cup breadcrumbs (homemade organic bread or organic bread put in blender)

1 tsp salt

1 cup of water

Oil for frying (Organic olive, avocado, peanut or any oil of your choice)

Mix all ingredients together

Form into 16 balls 2-3 inch balls. Chill until ready to fry

Fry in a skillet until browned all the way around

♥ Serve with spaghetti or on a hoagie roll

Roast Beef in Gravy

3 lbs. grass-fed free-range organic roast (no glued pieces/ transglutaminase)

1 can organic cream of mushroom soup

1 can of water

4-5 small potatoes or 2 large potatoes cut into quarters

2 large onions cut into quarters

2 large carrots cut chopped into pieces

In 13" x 8" glass baking dish, lined with a large piece of aluminum foil

Optional- pour a small amount of olive oil on the bottom

Place all ingredients in aluminum

Wrap aluminum foil over top and seal closed

Bake at 350 for 45 to 60 minutes depending on how well done you want it

Carefully unwrap meat and serve

Memories Make the Best Recipes

This is a recipe that came from MJ, a friend of mine, when I was first married. MJ gave me many recipes, which she had collected from other Army wives from all over the world. It had been one of my "fool-proof" favorite recipes for many years. Then something changed in the quality of meat and ingredients sold in my local grocery stores. Around the year 2008, when I baked it, the house no longer filled with its rich aroma; the meat was hard to cut and tasted awful.

After realizing genetically engineered meat products and those made from old pieces of meat glued together with transglutaminase do not work well with my old favorite recipes. Now that I am using only organic beef, this recipe is once again fool-proof.

Meat Loaf

2 Lb. Organic Ground Beef
2 Shredded carrots
Chopped onion
Chopped pepper
1 organic egg
¾ cup of organic breadcrumbs

Topping
½ cup Organic Ketchup
4Tbsp Mustard
2 Tbsp Truvia brown sugar
1/2 tsp nutmeg

Blend meat with ingredients. Place in a bread pan

Bake at 350 F for 40 minutes

In the meantime, mix topping ingredients in a bowl

Pour over meatloaf and cook an additional 20 minutes

Seafood

Avocado Shrimp Salsa

1 lb. boiled shrimp	3 Roma tomatoes
Salt and pepper	2 medium cucumbers
1 Tbsp avocado oil (or olive)	1 small-medium organic onion
3 medium limes	½ cup cilantro

Sauté shrimp in avocado oil with a dash of salt and pepper

Mix the rest of the chopped ingredients together.

Add shrimp mixture. Refrigerate for at least 2 hours

♥ Serve with tortilla chips.

Shrimp Cocktail Sauce

1 cup organic Ketchup	p of organic fresh lemon juice
1 Tbsp organic horseradish	p chopped organic onion
1 tsp Worcestershire Sauce	

Mix ingredients in a bullet or blender. Pour into a jar and refrigerate for at least 4 hours.

Spinach Fettuccini with Crabmeat Sauce

1 lb. spinach fettuccini boiled

6 organic scallions chopped

8 oz crab meat chopped

4 Tbsp organic butter

4 Tbsp olive oil

1 pint of heavy cream (100% cream with NO CARRAGEENAN)

2 fresh tomatoes cored & chopped

1/3 cup Chablis or cooking sherry

Parsley for garnish

Grated cheese for garnish

Cook pasta. Drain well, top with crabmeat sauce and garnish

Make the Sauce:

Heat oil in a large skillet over medium heat

Add scallions—heat 2 minutes

Add crabmeat, tomatoes, and butter. Cook 2 minutes

Add heavy cream and Chablis or cooking sherry. Stir for 3 minutes

Memories Make the Best Recipes

When my children were small, there was a fresh fish market one a back street in New Hope, Pa. They supplied the local restaurants with fresh wild-caught seafood and fish and sold a small amount to local people. I remember crabmeat being very cheap, and my family loved this recipe.

My son was adamantly against alcohol for some reason, so I didn't mention to him that this contained cooking sherry, which I think brings out the best flavor.

I tried to cook this recipe some time in the early 21st century, and it turned out awful every time. In retrospect, I now know that:

A. Imitation crab meat does not taste like the real thing

B. Heavy cream diluted with water and carrageenan does not thicken, and it causes a lot of stomach pains afterward

C. GMO scallions do not have the flavor of organic scallion.

Now that I only use organic ingredients, this recipe is once again flawless every time.

Red Clam Sauce over Linguini

¼ cup olive oil	3 cups organic crushed tomatoes
2 Tbsp butter	1 cup clam juice
¼ chopped onion	1 ¼ tsp salt
4 large garlic cloves minced	¾ lb. chopped clams
2/3 cup white wine (I use sweet)	1/3 cup parsley chopped
½ tsp thyme	¼ tsp ground pepper
Pinch red pepper	Linguini – boiled

Heat oil and butter in a large skillet, add onion and garlic and cook until soft—about 3 minutes

Add wine and thyme, reduce to 1/3rd cup

Add tomatoes & clam juice—simmer 10 minutes or until thickened

Add salt, chopped clams, parsley, and ground pepper. Simmer

Serve over Linguine

♥ Can be prepared the day before and refrigerated or frozen.

Hot Crab Dip

6 Tbsp organic cream cheese	4 Tbsp minced organic onion
½ cup organic mayonnaise	1 small garlic clove crushed
7 – 8 oz crabmeat	1 Tbsp lemon juice
¼ cup of shredded cheddar cheese	½ tsp hot pepper sauce

Preheat oven 350 F

Beat cream cheese and mayo until smooth.   Stir in rest of ingredients except cheese.

Grease oven-proof dish and spoon mixture into it.

Sprinkle with cheese.

Bake 20 minutes.

Serve with crackers or chips

Memories Make the Best Recipes

My son and I found this recipe on a postcard when our extended family shared two houses at Bethany Beach one summer. Rob and I prepared and served it as an appetizer one evening. It remained a favorite ever since.

Salmon in Garlic Butter

1 lb. wild-caught salmon	½ tsp oregano chopped
½ cup melted butter	½ tsp Thyme chopped
1 Tbsp Truvia Brown Sugar	½ tsp Rosemary chopped
1 Tbsp Lemon Juice	Salt & pepper
3 medium-sized garlic cloves minced	Parsley for garnish

Preheat oven to 375 F

Wash and pat dry the salmon and set aside.

Mix the rest of the ingredients. Coat bottom of the baking dish with olive or avocado oil.

Coat both sides of salmon with mixture. Pour half of the remaining mixture in the baking dish.

Place salmon in dish and pour the rest of the garlic sauce over the top. Put a sprig of parsley on each. Optional: put a slice of lemon on each. Cover baking dish with aluminum foil.

Bake 30 minutes

Salmon in Honey Mustard Sauce

1 ½ to 2 pounds fresh wild-caught salmon

3 Tbsp Honey Mustard (half honey + half Dijon mustard)

3 garlic cloves minced

Olive or Avocado Oil

1 Tbsp lemon juice

1 Tbsp fresh dill chopped

Salt

Preheat oven 400 F.

Coat bottom of the baking dish with olive or avocado oil.

Wash and pat dry salmon and put aside.

Mix all remaining ingredients together. Coat both sides of salmon. Place in baking dish.

Bake for 20 -30 minutes.

Poultry

I just completed this book when I realized I left out this section on poultry. How in the world could I leave this section out? I owned an Organic Poultry Farm back in 1978 – 1984, whereas I raised fresh chickens, turkeys, and eggs. And on the side, I gut and plucked chickens for other farmers. The fresh chicken was the main staple in our home.

Left-Over Turkey & Chicken Croquettes

2 Tbsp butter	1/4 cup minced onion
2 ½ Tbsp flour	2 Tbsp minced celery
1 cup milk	2 eggs beaten
2 cups minced chicken or turkey	1 cup breadcrumbs
(leftover)	1/8 tsp pepper
1 tsp salt	

Make white sauce with butter, flour, and milk in a pan until thickened.

Add chicken or turkey, veggies, and seasonings. Let cool in the refrigerator until thick and can be formed into 12 – 16 large balls.

Dip in crumbs, then beaten egg, and again in crumbs.

In a large frying pan, heat cooking oil—fry croquettes.

♥   Serve with gravy or ketchup

Chicken Divine

4 Boneless chicken breasts cut in half (Organic)—boiled

(save the juice for another recipe)

2 packages of frozen broccoli—lightly steamed or boiled

1 packet onion soup mix

1-pint sour cream (organic and no carrageenan)

1 cup heavy whipping cream (100% cream and no carrageenan)

Parmesan cheese

Lay all of the broccoli on the bottom of a shallow 13" x 8" baking dish.

Mix sour cream and soup mix. Spread ½ over broccoli

Place chicken on top of broccoli and sauce

Whip cream until thick, stir in remaining sour cream & soup mix. Spread over top of chicken.

Sprinkle with parmesan cheese

Bake at 375 F for 20 minutes

BBQ Chicken Legs in Crockpot

12 chicken legs	½ cup organic Ketchup
½ cup flour	½ cup vinegar
Dash of salt and pepper	½ chopped onion
½ cup Grandma Molasses	1 Tbsp Worcestershire Sauce

Mix flour, pepper, and salt together.

Rinse chicken, pat dry, and roll in flour mixture.

Place in crockpot.

Mix rest of ingredients together. Pour over chicken.

Cook on low for 6-7 hours.

Memories Make the Best Recipes:

This recipe is one I created from multiple recipes and turned out to be a family favorite. I could fill two crockpots and go off about my day and then have a wonderful dinner for my mother, brother's, and my family. It always tasted wonderful. Then one day, I made it for a potluck dinner in 2005, and it was awful—bitter and horrible. I tried to make it again a few more times, but each time it turned out bitter and awful. Recently I decided to try it once again but with all 100% organic ingredients—organic chicken, ketchup, onion, and flour. Much to my amazement, it tasted wonderful again. I repeated these ingredients again to make dinner for my good friends Skip and Mac—it was Mac's birthday, and the meal was fabulous. The proof is truly in the ingredients!

Vegetables

String Bean Casserole

2 12 oz can of Non-GMO organic green beans

2 12 oz cans of Non-GMO organic wax beans

8 oz Non-GMO mushrooms

8 oz Non-GMO tomato sauce

1-2 Tbsp organic butter

Parmesan cheese

Drain and blend together the beans and mushrooms.

Pour into an 8" x 4" x 3" bread-baking dish

Pour tomato sauce over top

Cut butter into small chunks and drop over the top

Sprinkle with parmesan cheese

Bake at 350 degrees for 20 minutes

♥ Makes great side dish

French Fries

Organic Russet potatoes

Oil: Peanut, Pecan, Avocado or Olive (can be a mixture of oils)

Optional: Salt

Serve with organic ketchup

Microwave potatoes on high of 1 minute

Slice into strips; sprinkle with salt if desired

Heat ½" to 1" of oil in a large skillet. Drop potato slices into pan, single layer at a time.

Fry until browned on both sides

Drain on a paper towel

Mashed potatoes (cream cheese)

Serving 4

4 large organic russet potatoes boiled until soft

2 oz. creamed cheese

Splash of milk and a dab of organic butter

Put all ingredients into a bowl. Blend well with mixer or handheld blender.

Transfer to serving dish.

♥ I saved the boiled potato liquid in the refrigerator until after the turkey dinner. It was then used to make leftover turkey soup.

♥ Make double portions and keep for leftovers. Often tastes better the next day.

♥ Save the liquid to boil other vegetables. It adds flavor to the other veggies, and it makes a great broth. It can be frozen in an ice cube tray and then saved on a larger container.

Memories Make the Best Recipes

I used to mash potatoes with a wire masher. Around the age of ten, my son complained that I made my mashed potatoes too lumpy, and therefore, that Thanksgiving, he decided to mash the potatoes. Grandma peeled a dozen or so potatoes and boiled them in a large pan. When they were soft, Grandma carefully transferred the soft potatoes into a large bowl and called Rob to come to mash and prepare the potatoes.

He ever so diligently mashed those potatoes until they were blended into a silky texture. He then added the creamed cheese, butter, and milk. He then spread it into a large serving dish, and we put it on the table ready for our friends and family.

As I finished up the turkey and made last-minute preparations, Grandma washed the dishes. She realized there was a potato left in the pan and asked me what she should do with it. We considered mashing it, then I thought about how much he complained about lumps in my mashed potatoes. What Mom and I did was bury the whole boiled potato inside Rob's dish of mashed potatoes and smoothed his mashed potatoes over it.

Everyone was then seated around the table when Ro stood up as proud as a peacock tapping his glass to get everyone's attention. "I made the mashed potatoes!" he explained. "My mashed potatoes are as smooth as a newborn baby's fanny!"

Miraculously, he stuck the serving fork directly into the hidden whole boiled potato and pulled out this huge lump. He was so puzzled when he blurted out, "How the heck…." He saw Grandma and me laughing and then said, "I can understand mom… but you-- Grandma. Why?"

Rob was such a good-natured child, and everyone laughed so hard when he retold this story at future meals.

Beet Tops

1 slice of bacon

¼ cup chopped onion

1 large garlic clove crushed

16 oz or so of chopped Beet leaves – remove woody stems, rinse well

¾ cup of water

1 Tbsp Truvia sugar

1 tsp red pepper flakes

3 Tbsp vinegar

Soak beet tops in water until ready to use

Fry bacon strip in a large frying pan, then chop into pieces

Add onion and garlic and fry until tender. If not enough bacon fat, add some olive oil.

Drain beet tops well, then add to the frying pan. Pour ¾ cup water over the top. Add sugar and pepper flakes. Boil and stir frequently until cooked.

Simmer for 10 minutes, then remove from heat and add vinegar.

Cauliflower Au Gratin

Head of cauliflower	1 slice of organic breadcrumbs
1organic Valencia onion	Splash of organic milk
4 Tbsp butter	Baby swiss cheese
4 Tbsp oil of your choice	

Boil Cauliflower until soft (If boiling potatoes for a meal, use the same water—it adds flavor)

Drain and mash cauliflower

Sauté' onion in butter and oil.

Add cauliflower to the onion. Add a splash of organic milk.

Pour into 8" x 4" baking dish.

Top with swiss cheese and bread-crumbs.

Bake 20 minutes

Desserts

Peanut Butter Chocolate Balls

In a double boiler- mix together:

    1/3 block of paraffin

    1 12 0z package chocolate chips

In a bowl, combine:

    ½ cup butter

    1 ½ cup chunky or smooth peanut butter

    2 cups sifted 10xx sugar

    ** choice: coconut or Rice Krispies – enough to make firm

Refrigerate until chocolate mixture is cool and firm

Roll into about 50 balls

Roll in chocolate paraffin until well coated (use toothpicks to hold balls)

Place on wax paper

Memories Make the Best Recipes

In the first year of my marriage, my husband and I were close friends with a couple named MJ and Richie. Richie worked with my husband. MJ and I were housewives. She was divorced from a retired career military man. During those years, MJ had collected many recipes that she then shared with me. Once a week, she cooked dinner, and once a week, I cooked something that I researched and created.

This Peanut Butter Ball recipe became a family favorite. My mom began making them for every family event. And recently, I learned that my brother made them for friends and family every Christmas. Then by coincidence, my childhood best friend texted me a recipe card she copied from my mom's recipe book.

Kudos to MJ—this recipe awed many of my friends and family!

Millie's Strawberry Pie

1 organic pre-made pie crust or make your own

1 pint (6 cups) fresh organic strawberries

1 cup of sugar

3 tablespoons cornstarch

1/2 cup water

1-pint whipping cream (100% cream: NO CARRAGEENAN or diluted with water)

1 /2 cup Organic 10x sugar

Bake pie crust as directed and cool

Meanwhile, in a small bowl, crush enough strawberries to make 1 cup

In 2-quart saucepan, mix sugar and cornstarch; stir in crushed strawberries and water

Cook, constantly stirring until mixture boils and thickens

Cool completely, about 30 minutes

Place remaining strawberries, whole or sliced, in the cooled baked shell. Pour cooked strawberry mixture evenly over berries. Refrigerate until set, about 3 hours, before serving

Just before serving to make whipped cream. Mix whipped cream unto thick and forms peaks, gently mix in 10x sugar

♥ Either spoon whipped cream onto the top of the pie just before serving or put a bowl of whipped cream on the side for guests to put on themselves.

♥ Use only whipped cream made from 100% cream. Whipped cream that is diluted with water and carrageenan does not whip up nicely and may cause some guests to have irritable bowel symptoms after eating

Memories Make the Best Recipes

This is a recipe my granddaughter and I made up together. She was staying overnight one weekend when we visited a local organic strawberry farm. We picked a lot of juicy sweet strawberries, then looked up a few recipes that we combined into one recipe.

We made this pie again for a party at my best friend's house in New Hampshire. Millie sliced the strawberries and mixed the ingredients. Later that day, she ever so proudly told guests she made the pie. It was the most adorable thing to watch as the pie got completely devoured.

Ginger Cookies

2 ¼ High Gluten Non-GMO flour	¾ cup soft butter
2 tsp grated ginger	½ cup Truvia sugar
1 tsp baking soda	1 egg
¾ tsp ground cinnamon	¼ cup molasses
½ tsp ground cloves	1 Tbsp water
¼ tsp salt	1 Tbsp Truvia sugar

Preheat oven 350 F

In bowl mix first six ingredients and set aside

In another bowl, beat butter. Add sugar and egg and beat until light and fluffy. Beat in molasses and water.

Gradually mix in flour mixture.

Make 2 Tbsp size balls and roll in remaining sugar.

Place on ungreased cookie sheet 2 " apart. Bake for 10 minute

Memories Make the Best Recipes

My dad loved ginger snap cookies dipped in his coffee. He would have loved this recipe. When I make ginger cookies, I too enjoy dunking them in coffee—even though I don't drink hot coffee.

Dog Food

Human food is not the only thing that has changed since the 1990s. The technology of Mechanically Separated Meat (MSM) and Mechanically Retrieved Meat (MRM) processing enables food processors to use these scraps of meat (once reserved for pet food) in human food. Hence, pet food in the past (made from meat scraps) has been replaced with chemicals. Modern pet foods sold today are loaded with chemicals and fillers that didn't use to be in pet foods. Many of these chemicals and fillers are causing human diseases in our pets, while others are downright unsafe for pet consumption. **In July 2018, the FDA began investigating reports of increased heart disease leading to canine dilated cardiomyopathy. A link between diet and heart disease was identified (FDA, 2018).**

One example of an additive with no nutritional value is Carrageenan, which is common in pet food – it is a bulking agent that causes digestive issues, increases the amount of stool produced and causes cancer (Tobacman, 2001); food dyes have no nutritional value but can cause behavioral problems and cancer in pets (Potera, 2010), (Arnold, 2012),

In fact, specific food-grade dyes cause specific health problems in dogs that can lead to very high veterinarian fees to reverse the damage (the cure is to remove the causing agent. Research shows:

- ¤ Violet, Blue, and Green Dye— autoimmune deficiency and digestive problems (Hess, 1955)
- ¤ **Blue #2 – cancer, brain tumors, and allergic reactions (Gaines Family Farmstead, 2017)**

- ¤ Brilliant Red and Red Dye #40—liver & kidney failure, urinary tract dysfunction, premature death (Davis, 1966); Hyperactivity in pets (Tobacman, 2001)
- ¤ Yellow Dye #5 -- neurochemical and behavioral effects, including hyperactivity, aggression, and insomnia. It is also linked to asthma, allergies, thyroid tumors, lymphomas, ADHD, and chromosomal damage (Gaines Family Farmstead, 2017)
- ¤ Yellow Dye #6 -- adrenal gland and kidney tumors, skin issues, asthma, and chromosomal damage (Gaines Family Farmstead, 2017)

There are many more chemicals with many other side-effects, which is why I make my own homemade dog food. Whereas leftovers may not meet my pet's nutritional needs, I look for nutrients balanced recipes. If you choose to cook for your dog, animal care professionals agree that you should use nutritionally complete recipes.

I typically make a batch that lasts 7 – 14 days, and I freeze the individual portions. Using a slow-cooker, it only takes 5 minutes to prepare, and then it cooks while I sleep.

John and I buy only kibbles with no dyes and have the least chemicals with the first ingredients being real meat.

Basic Dog Food Recipe

2 pounds of organic ground beef, turkey or chicken

¼ cup sunflower, olive or other non-GMO oil

1 cup of boiled brown rice

1 can organic black beans- rinsed

A mixture of boiled carrots, broccoli, or peas- blend in Nutra Bullet

Fry meat and oil in a pan. Boil rice. Boil vegetables and then add rice and beans to vegetables. Add meat

Memories Make the Best Recipes

This is the basic dog food recipe I have used for years. I always use healthy organic ingredients, so I knew it was healthy and safe for consumption. When I traveled, I used to leave my dog Sadie with a friend. Often I brought baked goodies for her too. During one of my trips, she called me to ask why I didn't leave any dog food for Sadie and wanted to know what she should feed my dog. I was confused because I left a large bowl of organic turkey with rice and vegetables. After a moment or so, I told her just to buy something. Before hanging up that evening, she thanked me for the delicious turkey, rice, and broccoli I left for her. She said it was enough for two meals.

LOL, I suppose organic ingredients are wonderful for everyone!

Slow Cooker Recipe

2 -3 lbs. boneless chicken breasts or thighs

1 sweet potato cubes

2 carrots sliced – leave the skin on as this contains many nutrients

2 cups fresh or frozen string beans

2 cups fresh or frozen peas

1 large non-GMO apple – remove core and seeds, slice into pieces

1 can of non-GMO kidney or white beans

2 Tbsp organic oil

4 cups of water or organic chicken broth

Put all ingredients into a slow cooker

Cook on slow for 6 – 8 hours. Let food, chop, or blend into small consistency.

Put in one portion size dishes and freeze

Slow Cooker Beef Stew

2 1/2 pounds ground beef

1 (15 oz.) can kidney beans, rinsed and drained

1 1/2 cups brown rice

1 1/2 cups butternut squash, chopped into small cubes

1 1/2 cups carrots, finely chopped

3/4 cup peas, fresh or frozen

4 cups of water or (3 cups water and 1 cup organic beef broth)

Place all ingredients into a slow cooker, stir, cover, and cook on slow for 6 hours.

Cool, divide into single portion containers, and freeze

Bacon & Peanut Butter Biscuits

1 cup Organic Peanut Butter

¾ cup of organic milk

1 egg or 1 cup of apple sauce or 1 cup puree pumpkin

2 cups whole wheat flour

1 Tbsp baking powder

¾ cup organic oats

3 fried bacon strips chopped— (Optional -- reserve

    the bacon fat & add to the recipe).

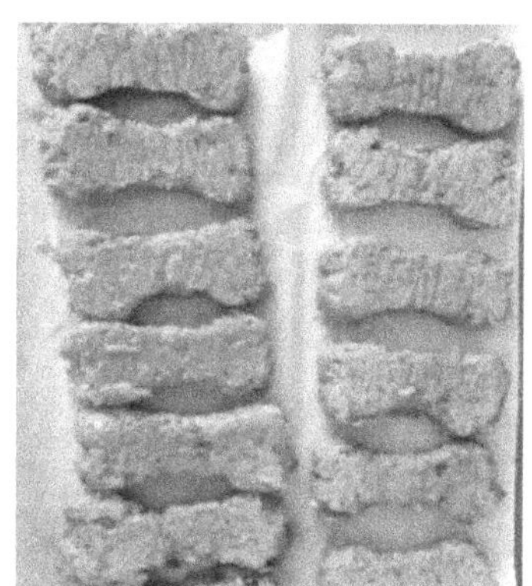

Preheat oven at 325 F

Line cookie sheets with parchment paper

Cook the bacon until golden and crisp. Allow cooling then cut into small pieces.

In a bowl using a whisk, blend together the peanut butter, milk, an egg, or applesauce.

Sift in the flour and baking powder and stir this through until a dough forms

Mix in the bacon (bacon fat if desired) and oats, so they are evenly distributed.

Roll the dough out to desired thickness, use cookie cutters (I use a dog-bone shaped cutter)

Place on the baking tray, close together as they do not spread.

Bake 15 minutes, then remove from oven and flip each biscuit over and cook again for 10 minutes

Allow cooling thoroughly. It can be stored in an airtight container at room temperature or in the freezer

Conclusion

Whether you use my recipes or your own, when cooking with hormone-free, chemical-free, Non-GMO, organic ingredients, you'll notice a big difference. It may take a few weeks for your health to improve (until you get the chemicals out of your system), but the difference in the taste of your homemade meals will be instant!

Although I shared a few of my favorite recipes, the main purpose of this book is to emphasize the importance of the quality of ingredients used. Today, more than ever before, what we put into our recipes affects our health in so many ways. Try preparing your favorite recipes with ingredients that are hormone-free, chemical-free, Non-GMO, and organic to see for yourself the difference in quality, texture, and taste.

I hope readers understand-- *if your cooking isn't great*--- there's a good chance it is the ingredients, and it has nothing to do with your skills for cooking.

Also, please look up the references I used because there is so much more information in each reference.

Please feel free to send me any comments or short quips about your own experiences with GMO vs. Non-GMO and other processed ingredients. You can send your comments to Rebekah@whatseatingyou.info

If you send me comments or a short (few paragraphs about your experiences with ingredients and your recipes, please include a note stating whether or not I can publish your letter in a future book).

REFERENCES

Arnold, L. l. (2012). Artificial food colors and Attention-Deficit/Hyperactivity Symptoms: Conclusions to dye for. *Neurotherapeutics*, 599 - 609.

CALPRIG. (2011). *Apples to Twinkies.* Retrieved from CALIFORNIA PUBLIC INTEREST RESEARCH GROUP (CALPRIG): https://calpirg.org/reports/cap/apples-twinkies

Charrez, B. Q. (2015). The role of fructose in metabolism and cancer. *Hormone Mol Biol Clin Investig.22(2)*, 79-89.

Dannie, M. (2018). *The health benefits of high gluten flour.* Retrieved from sAFEGATE (sf): https://healthyeating.sfgate.com/health-benefits-high-gluten-flour-11987.html

David, S. S.-H. (2018). Revisiting the carrageenan controversy: do we really understand the digestive fate and safety of carrageenan in our foods? *Food Funct. 9(3)*, 1344-1352.

Davis, K. N. (1966). Chronic toxicity of ponceau SX to rats, mice, and dogs. *Toxicology and Pharmacology, 8 (2)*, 306-317.

Di Nardo G1, V. M. (2019). Nutritional deficiencies in children with Celiac Disease Resulting from a gluten-Free diet: A systematic review. *Nutrients 11(7)*, 1 - 12.

EFSA. (1993). Scientific opinion on the public health risks related to mechanically separated meat and mechanically retrieved meat derived from poultry and swine. *Europian Food Safety Authority Journal (EFSA)*, 1-78.

FDA. (2018). *FDA investigation into the potential link between certain diets and canine dilated cardiomyopathy.* Retrieved from Food & Drug Administration: In July 2018, the FDA announced that it had begun investigating reports of canine dilated cardiomyopathy (DCM) in dogs eating certain pet foods

Gaines Family Farmstead. (2017). *Why You Should Avoid Artificial Food Coloring in Dog Treats.* Retrieved from Gaines Family Farmstead:

https://gainesfamilyfarmstead.com/blogs/news/why-you-should-avoid-artificial-food-coloring-in-dog-treats

Hess, S. F. (1955). Absorption and excretion of certain triphenylmethane colors in rats and dogs. *Journal of Pharmacology and Experimental Therapeutics, 114(1)*, 38 - 42.

Kupper, C. (2005). Dietary guidelines and implementation for celiac disease. *Gastroenterology 128*, S121.

Martin, J., Geisel, T., Maresch, C., Krieger, K., & Stein, J. (2013). Inadequate nutrient intake in people with celiac disease. Results from a German survey. *Digestion 240e6*, 87.

Potera, C. (2010). Diet and nutrition: The artificial dye in food blues. *Environmental Health Perspectives 118(10)*, A428.

The Cornucopia Institute. (2010). *Federal subsidies for commodity crops are also subsidizing junk food additives.* Retrieved from The Cornucopia Institute: https://www.cornucopia.org/2011/09/report-taxpayer-subsidies-for-junk-food-wasting-billions/

Tobacman, K. (2001). Review of harmful gastrointestinal effects of carrageenan in animal experiments. *Environmental Health Perspectives 109(10)*, 983–994.

Topsakal, S. O. (2016). Alpha-lipoic acid attenuates high-fructose-induced pancreatic toxicity. *Pancreatology 16(3)*, 347-352.

Wozencraft, B. (2019). *10 reasons why organic costs more.* Retrieved from LowTox Living,com: https://www.low-toxliving.com/where-to-start#!

Meet the Author

Rebekah Sue Mead, RN, BSN, MSN Ed., FND, CHWC, COAHC, has been a patient advocate and educator for more than thirty years. She passionately promotes self-efficacy and public awareness. She considers good health and quality of life to be the same—they are achievable, and everyone's responsibility.

As an advocate and educator, Rebekah wants everyone to know that we do not have to rely on legislation and medicine to keep us healthy— our lifestyle is our choice. By purchasing only healthy hormone & chemical-free, Non-GMO, organic foods, we as consumers can end the harmful effects of processed foods saturated in pesticides by simply not allowing these products in our living spaces.

Rebekah grew up on a farm in Stockton, NJ. It is there that her love for gardening and eating healthy evolved. In 1978, Rebekah established her own organic chicken business—she sold organic chicken and turkeys, and chicken eggs.

Rebekah earned an associate degree in nursing from the Raritan Valley Community College. There the instructors and nursing curriculum emphasized holistic nursing care. Being a natural historian, Rebekah revered Florence Nightingale's foundation of modern nursing. The articles by Florence Nightingale influenced Rebekah's confidence in fresh (unpolluted) air, exercise, and clean food as the basis of good health and quality of life.

Rebekah earned a Forensic Nurse Diploma (FND) from Kaplan University. She then went on to earn her bachelor's and masters' degrees in Nursing education from the Thomas Edison State College of NJ. Her electives included the biology of nutrition. After graduating from TESC, Rebekah became an occupational- environmental health and safety nurse. This experience brought together all of her experience and education in environmental health. As an Environmental Health and Safety Nurse, Rebekah learned the value of a root-cause-analysis—she identified risks and then worked with a team of safety engineers to eliminate or mitigate the causing agent. She now applies this to food safety. When research shows potential risks, those at the highest risk should eliminate those additives and products completely from their diets; anyone not at high risk should be aware of potential symptoms that empower consumers to decide for themselves if they want to take those risks or not.

Now living in Florida, Rebekah published her first book in 2019 -- What's Eating You? A Food Reference Manual. Currently, she speaks on the radio and lectures about eating healthy. When asked how she avoids hormones, food additives, GMO and pesticides--- she replies, "I eat everything I used to eat using organic ingredients."

Rebekah's second book, *Naturally Delicious,* explains how to eat healthy without sacrificing the foods you love.

Rebekah Mead is the author of What's Eating You? A food reference manual – In her first book, she explains how the food you eat today becomes the vital supplies your body uses to maintain your health. The last chapter lists multiple chemicals and their side-effects—if you experience symptoms of illness after eating a meal, avoid the chemicals that may be causing or at least contributing to those symptoms.